Northamptons
Stories

Northamptonshire Stories

Marian Pipe

With Illustrations by Eve Dymond-White

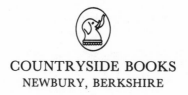

COUNTRYSIDE BOOKS
NEWBURY, BERKSHIRE

First Published 1995
© Marian Pipe 1995

COUNTRYSIDE BOOKS
3 Catherine Road
Newbury, Berkshire

ISBN 1 85306 355 X

*To Angie, who loves
history as much as I do*

Designed by Mon Mohan

Produced through MRM Associates Ltd, Reading
Typeset by Paragon Typesetters, Clwyd
Printed by J.W. Arrowsmith Ltd., Bristol

Contents

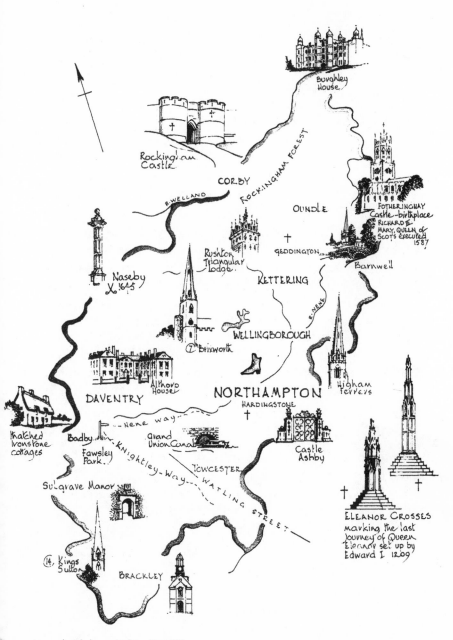

Burghley House

Rockingham Castle

CORBY

R.WELLAND

ROCKINGHAM FOREST

OUNDLE

FOTHERINGHAY Castle - birthplace RICHARD III MARY, QUEEN of Scots executed 1587

Naseby X 1645

Rushton Triangular Lodge

GEDDINGTON

Barnwell

KETTERING

R.NENE

WELLINGBOROUGH

Brixworth

Althorp House

DAVENTRY

NORTHAMPTON

HARDINGSTONE

Higham Ferrers

Thatched Ironstone cottages

Badby

Fawsley Park.

Nene way

Grand Union Canal

Knightley Way

Towcester

Castle Ashby

WATLING STREET

Sulgrave Manor

ELEANOR CROSSES marking the last Journey of Queen Eleanor set up by Edward I 1209

14. Kings Sutton

BRACKLEY

© map designed and drawn by PENNY VEYS 1994

Acknowledgements

I WOULD like to thank the following people for the help they have given me in the compiling of this book: Doreen Allen of Woodford, David Balentine of Geddington, Q. Bland of Grafton Underwood, A. Buksh of Kettering, Dr Trevor Hopkins, Headmaster of Bishop Stopford School, Kettering, H.J. Johnson of Irthlingborough, Dorothy Lewin of Woodford, John Letch of Corby, Bernard Moore (Mr Woo), Jean Parker of Rothwell, Hazel Payne of Kettering, Helen Rowland of Woodnewton, Mr and Mrs Russell Jenner of Woodnewton, Alice Smith of Kettering, Gordon Wells of Isham.

My grateful thanks, too, to the staff at Kettering Library, especially Malcolm Robinson who knows the local history section so well, and to the staff at the Central Library, Abington Street, Northampton.

I would also like to acknowledge the help given to me by the staff of the *Northamptonshire Evening Telegraph*.

1

A Fateful Meeting

WHEN Elizabeth Grey waylaid Edward IV in the forest of Whittlebury (now Whittlewood Forest) it could be said that she changed the course of history. She certainly set the Woodvilles on the road to great wealth and power.

The King was riding out alone on a day's hunting, when Elizabeth, eldest daughter of Sir Richard Woodville and Jacquetta of Luxembourg, stopped him and begged him to clear the name of her late husband, Sir John Grey, a Lancastrian knight who had fallen in battle and on whom a dreaded bill of attainder had been passed.

Edward fell in love with her and shortly afterwards they married in secret, in May 1464, in the manor house at Grafton Regis, the family home of the Woodvilles. Elizabeth was generally thought to be a very unsuitable choice of bride for the King. For not only was she a commoner and a widow with two young sons, but also she was five years older than him. The powerful Earl of Warwick, known as the Kingmaker, had already made plans to push Edward into a diplomatic marriage with Bona of Savoy, a French princess. However, Edward had Elizabeth crowned on Whit Sunday in 1465. The Woodvilles were showered with undeserved honours and the Queen's relatives were able to make very advantageous marriages. All of which angered Warwick.

Edward found out, like his predecessors, that the royal

revenues did not stretch far enough to meet his royal expenditure. He called in the coinage and reminted it, reducing the silver content by 20 per cent. This upset the merchants, who believed that they were getting a bad deal by getting less value for the gold and silver that they handed in. Plotting and treason were rife and there was great unrest in the country, with armed uprisings in the north and the Isle of Wight. Warwick was in open defiance when his daughter, Isabel, was married to the Duke of Clarence, the King's brother, on the 11th July 1469.

In Lancashire, a rebellion was instigated by Warwick's agents and led by a man calling himself Robin of Redesdale, who was probably Sir John Conyers, whose wife Alice was the Earl of Warwick's cousin. Robin's chief lieutenants were Sir Henry Neville and Sir John Sutton. The intention was to end the influence of the Woodvilles, and the rebels hurriedly set off for Grafton Regis.

The King was waiting at Nottingham for reinforcements from the west. He had directed Lord Herbert, who had recently been raised to Earl of Pembroke, to lead all the forces he could muster in Wales against the rebels. They were joined on the way by another detachment, led by Humphrey, Lord Stafford of Southwick. Together they proceeded to Banbury, where there was a dispute between Herbert and Stafford over their quarters and the favour of a girl. Herbert won and Stafford withdrew his forces, which included most of the archers. It has been said that had Stafford not defected at that particular time, the outcome of the conflict at Edgecote might have had a different ending for the Yorkists.

The two opposing armies met up with one another on the field of Danesmoor, in the parish of Edgecote, which is 15 miles west of Grafton Regis. The royalist army drove the rebels from a hill overlooking the plain and up another hill, near to the village of Culworth. But the Lancastrians successfully held them off and each side withdrew to settle down for the night. Whilst under cover of darkness, Robin's men moved surreptitiously along the ridge and camped on the other side of the hill and out of sight of the Yorkist army. Lord Stafford and his defecting archers spent the night only 12 miles away from Edgecote.

On the morning of 26th July 1469, the rebels crossed the plateau to the royalist camp and took them by surprise, for the Earl of Pembroke had been expecting an attack from the east and not from the west. The royalists were forced down the hill by Robin's men onto Danesmoor. However, Herbert and his brother, Sir Richard Herbert, twice broke through the ranks of the enemy with their pole-axes and returned safely.

Then an event occurred which turned the battle in the favour of the rebels. A body of men was seen mounting up the eastern hill. Unfortunately for William Herbert, it wasn't the expected Stafford and his archers but John Chapman, a retainer of Warwick's, with 500 followers. In front of them was displayed the banner of the Earl of Warwick with his insignia of the White Bear. The Lancastrian supporters raised a shout of 'Warwick, Warwick,' and the Welshmen in the royal detachment thought that the great Earl himself was with the force, and fled in terror. The rebels followed, and slew a great number of them.

The Earl of Pembroke and his brother, Sir Richard, were captured and taken to Northampton, where they were executed in the market square. The King did not hear of the disaster until the 29th July, just after he had left Nottingham and was on his way to Grafton in a desperate attempt to save his wife's relations. But Edward was taken prisoner himself at Olney. Lord Rivers, the Queen's father, and Sir John Woodville, her brother, were captured at Chepstow and taken to Coventry where they were beheaded. Lord Stafford was put to death at Bridgwater.

The King was conducted to Warwick Castle and, shortly afterwards, was taken to Middleham. Although the power of the Woodvilles had been curtailed, Warwick's ruthless use of the axe on his opponents made him very unpopular and he was not in full control of the country. By September the King was set free and was once again at the head of his realm.

2

Sulgrave Manor Lives On!

WHO could imagine, as they look at Sulgrave Manor House today, that the ancestral home of George Washington, first President of the United States, so nearly became a ruin?

The attractive village of Sulgrave is the setting for this charming two-storied dwelling, built of warm, brown limestone and dating back to the 16th century – a perfect example of a small Tudor manor of Shakespeare's time. It is set in well-tended grounds, with a sundial from 1579 in the centre of the rose garden. The Washington coat of arms, to be seen in the main doorway in the spandrel, consists of three mullets and two bars, and these are thought to be the original stars and stripes of the American national flag. The Washington family lived at the house for nearly 120 years, from 1540-1657.

Lawrence Washington, who is recognised as the founder of the Sulgrave Washingtons, was born in Warton, in the county of Lancashire, around 1500. He was the eldest son of John, who came from an ancient northern family, and Margaret, who was the daughter of Robert Kytson and sister of Sir Robert Kytson, the great Tudor merchant. In 1529, Lawrence was acting as bailiff to William, Lord Parr of Horton, uncle of Catherine Parr, the last of Henry VIII's wives. Lord Parr owned land in Northamptonshire, as his wife, Mary Salisbury, was heiress of Horton, which was six miles from Northampton.

Lawrence was sent down to Northamptonshire on business by his patron, and married Elizabeth Gough in about 1530. She was a wealthy widow and her dowry bought Lawrence a town house in Northampton and the ownership of the rectories of Chelveston, Caldicote and Higham Ferrers. Lawrence probably took over the business interests of Elizabeth's deceased husband, who had been a prosperous trader in the county town. Immediately after the marriage, he left his position as Lord Parr's bailiff and was soon chosen to become a member of Northampton Borough Corporation. He became the Mayor of Northampton in 1532. The second time he became Mayor was in 1545 and he was at various times an Alderman and Justice of the Peace.

In 1538 Lawrence purchased the manor of Sulgrave from the Crown and land in nearby villages that had belonged to the priory of St Andrews in Northampton before its dissolution. His first wife died childless soon after this and he married for the second time, another widow, Amy Thomson, the daughter of Robert Pargeter of the neighbouring village of Greatworth. Lawrence and Amy had eleven children, seven daughters and four sons, and the manor house was probably built to accommodate their ever-increasing family. Lawrence and his wife lived a very comfortable life there. His business in the woolstapling trade flourished and he seems to have been on good terms with his important relations, the Kytsons. His kinswoman Katherine Kytson married John Spencer of Althorp and came to live in Northamptonshire in 1545, which connected the Washingtons to one of the greatest families in the county.

Lawrence Washington died a rich man on the 19th February 1584 and was buried in the 14th-century parish church of Sulgrave, as was his eldest son, Robert, later.

Robert Washington was born at Sulgrave Manor and lived there until his death in 1619. His own son, Lawrence, became an agent for the Spencer family and was buried at Great Brington, a village near Althorp. His son (yet another Lawrence) was born at Sulgrave and became rector of Purleigh in Essex. It was Rev Lawrence Washington's son, John who emigrated to America in 1656, and settled in Virginia. In 1732 his great-grandson, George Washington, was born.

By the 19th century, the manor, after passing through various hands, had degenerated into a shabby farmhouse and, in the 1890s, it even stood empty for a time. During 1914 plans were made for the celebrating of the 100 years peace between Britain and the USA since the end of the Anglo-American war but, because of the onset of the First World War, most of the proposals had to be abandoned. However, one of the objects that was achieved was the purchase of Sulgrave Manor by a British committee for the improvement of transatlantic friendship. Although the house was bought for the sum of £8,400 and the committee had raised £12,000 this was not sufficient to include its renovation, so after the war, a list of subscribers was opened and the name of HM King George V topped it. By this method a further £8,500 was added to the fund, to which the Americans had given £2,500, and the work of restoration, which had been entrusted to Sir Reginald Blomfield RA could now go ahead.

The refurbished house was first opened in 1921, and it has remained so ever since, largely due to the generosity and foresight of a group of ladies descended from men of the 13 colonies which originally formed the United States. The National Society of the Colonial Dames of America set themselves a target of $100,000 for a fund to be set up in 1924 to endow Sulgrave Manor in perpetuity. This figure was surpassed and, after 35,000 subscribers were obtained, the total came to $112,000. Fortunately for Sulgrave Manor, the Colonial Dames were obviously well advised in 1924, for their endowments are the manor's only source of regular, capital income.

Lawrence Washington's manor house, a happy family home in his lifetime, is again cherished, and is a continuing memorial to his most illustrious descendant.

3

A Hiding Place in Brampton Ash

IN Godfrey Anstruther's excellent book, *Vaux of Harrowden* there is a fascinating account of an affray in Kettering's market square in 1576, and from this event on one spring day we get an intriguing glimpse into a time of religious turmoil in the county's past.

Henry Norwich was very unpopular with the local Catholics in this area, for he informed against them to the authorities. As often happens at such times, families became divided by their different beliefs. This occurred in Henry's case – he was a 'Queen's man', but his nephews, Simon, Edward and Peter, remained staunch Catholics.

On Friday, 13th April 1576, Henry decided to visit Kettering Market, where he got the shock of his life. for suddenly he was attacked on all sides by men armed with daggers, staves and buckles. He received many blows to his head, shoulders and arms, which left him with great sores and wounds. The victim considered himself lucky to get away with his life and he was even more upset when he found out that one of the culprits was his nephew Edward. Henry insisted that the affray in Kettering Market was a planned affair by the local papists, Sir Thomas Tresham being involved as well as some of Lord Mordant's servants and Edward's brother Simon. Sir Thomas, however, protested that he was only drawing his sword to keep the peace. Edward was sued by his uncle for assault. The case was brought before William, Lord Vaux, with Sir Edward Brudenell and Sir John Spencer, at the Michaelmas Quarter Sessions in 1577, held at Northampton. Edward only admitted giving Henry a light blow with a stave. We do not know what the outcome was, but Henry was not satisfied and repeated his allegations before the Star Chamber the following year.

He also claimed that he had suffered many injustices in the past from those papists, saying that they had prevented the case being heard earlier by procuring his arrest on the charge that he had stolen a surplice from the church at Brampton Ash. It is at this point that Henry laid the blame for most of his ills at the door of his other nephew, Simon Norwich, who lived at Brampton Ash. He accused Simon of many more serious offences, such as defacing the English bible and using a Latin bible instead. He also claimed that his nephew supported a popish scholar at Louvain and had never been to church since Elizabeth had been crowned Queen, 'unless' Henry added, 'it was to the hermitage in the woods near to his house, where sometimes there were vagrant persons known to be priests where he heareth mass.' Many witnesses said that he had a chalice, an altar, a vestment and a mass book. The most serious crime to be disclosed in court was that Simon Norwich had been harbouring four old priests in the 'Hermitage'. These Catholic clergymen, named Newman, Oliver, Francis Donne and Collier, were disguised in the livery of Simon's servants.

Henry won his case and Simon was sent to Marshalsea prison on the 26th February 1578, and in the following February he was removed to the Fleet. His uncle was instructed to procure the arrest of the priests Collier and Donne, but was unsuccessful.

The hermitage in the wood, which was a mile from Brampton Ash, was well known in the district. In earlier days it was called the Hermitage of Bestor and dedicated to St Augustine of Canterbury. Pilgrims flocked to the centre and many sick people were said to be cured of their diseases. The last hermit to live there was called Chambers, and after he was turned out Simon Norwich took possession of the property. He rented it for the sum of ten shillings a year to Thomas Colwell and his wife, who had been driven out of their house at Faversham in Kent by religious persecution.

In 1580 a commission was set up for the purpose of discovering 'concealed land', which meant church land that had never reached the Queen. Henry drew the attention of the commission to the hermitage, but Simon Norwich had succeeded in buying it, and the Colwells and their eight children continued to live there for several more years without interference from the authorities. They were also able to take in a great number of priests. Their peaceful existence was disrupted in 1587 when a priest named Mountford Scot arrived at their door. He was destined to die a martyr. This priest objected to Thomas Colwell living in a religious house and said to him 'Get ye forth of this house, as fast as ye can, for I never knew any lay folks that dwell in religious houses but their ends were either hersy or beggery.'

Colwell became very upset at this verbal attack and went on a pilgrimage to Canterbury, where he walked round the walls of the cathedral to make atonement to St Augustine. He and his family were offered a dwelling at Rushton by Sir Thomas Tresham, but unfortunately Colwell was arrested on his way to London and sent to the new Fleet prison in October 1589. He was released in the following spring and was able to return to the hermitage, where he helped his wife and children to move to their new home at Rushton. His freedom was shortlived, however, for the very next day he had to return to prison. Colwell was to die three years later whilst incarcerated in the Fleet.

The hermitage, which stood to the south of Brampton Ash on the edge of what is now the busy A6 between Desborough and Market Harborough, and at the corner of the lane which leads to Brampton Ash, (possibly close to present day Hermitage Wood or The Hermitage), was probably demolished before the adjacent chapel which we know was demolished at the end of the 17th century.

4

The Secret Room at Harrowden Hall

THE ancient seat of the Vaux family, from the early 15th century until the end of the 17th century, was Harrowden Hall in the small village of Great Harrowden, two miles from Wellingborough. This was one of the leading recusant families in the country, with a history of violence and intrigue, and in the 16th century the Hall became a place of refuge for Catholic priests.

Elizabeth had married George, 3rd Baron Vaux, in 1585, but within nine years George had died, leaving her with six children under the age of eight. Wilful and proud, she was also a staunch supporter of the Catholic cause and wanted to set up a priest college at her home. In 1598 the well-known Jesuit Father John Gerard was sent as chaplain to Elizabeth in another of the Vaux's houses, this one in Irthlingborough. Because of the careless gossip of some of the servants, the authorities searched the entire building for the priest. He was able to escape but it became obvious that another property would have to be found, as a safer refuge for the priest and to create the kind of college Lady Vaux had in mind. They needed a much larger residence and, after looking at many houses in the county, they came across what they sought in Kirby Hall, near Corby. It was an immense place, surrounded by gardens and orchards, and seemed to be ideal for Elizabeth's purpose. It was leased on her behalf by Thomas

Mulsho of Finedon, who was one of the trustees for her young son, Edward, Lord Vaux.

In the year of 1599, Father Gerard arrived at Kirby Hall to inspect the building, with the view of moving in soon. He had taken with him Nicholas Owen, a crippled carpenter, who was very clever at constructing priest holes, with the object of examining the house and building such a hiding place at Kirby. Then Gerard returned to the old house at Irthlingborough, leaving Owen and another man, Hugh Sheldon, to get on with the job. Unfortunately, as Gerard and his party were returning to Lord Vaux's house, they were seen passing through Kettering. The officials were notified and a body of men was sent over to search Kirby Hall, but the building was too large for it to be surrounded completely and Owen was able to slip out through the cordon. Sheldon was not so lucky and got caught. He was taken to gaol but later sent into exile.

After this event, Elizabeth Vaux reluctantly decided that there was no alternative but to use the house at Harrowden as her base for helping Catholic priests. Although it was dilapidated and in need of major repair, the Vaux family and Father Gerard moved into the Hall. Lady Vaux had a separate three-storied wing built for the priests, next to the old chapel, which gave easy access for them to come and go as they pleased without being seen. Meanwhile, Nicholas Owen got down to work, constructing hiding places at Harrowden Hall. One source of information gives the new wing that Elizabeth built for the priests as a place where Owen constructed a priest hole. If so, it was probably the only time that he was able to incorporate a design as part of an original building. Another writer says that on the stable block (which is still standing) there was a further hiding place, positioned between the floors.

Elizabeth was able to help many priests at her home at Harrowden and it became a well-known meeting place for

Catholics. Then, in November 1605, after the discovery of the gunpowder plot, she came under suspicion again for harbouring Father Gerard. The Earl of Salisbury gave orders that the priest should be captured at all costs. William Tate and a party of 100 well-armed soldiers were dispatched to Harrowden Hall, to perform the task of scouring the building until the priest was found.

When they arrived at Great Harrowden on Tuesday, 12th November, patrols were placed on every road within a three mile radius and guards set up around the house. Then the search began in earnest. Tate demanded the keys from Lady Vaux and gathered all the servants together. Elizabeth and her son Edward, who was only 17 at the time, were co-operative and remained very calm. Tate and his soldiers examined everywhere very thoroughly and then each room was locked and the keys handed personally to Tate. They ransacked coffers of linen, turned over trunks of clothing and pushed candles into every crevice. Elizabeths's closet was searched for letters that might supply them with evidence to incriminate Father Gerard of treason.

In the meantime, the priest was hiding in 'Owen's secret room' – a hole within a hole. He was a tall man and, although he could sit down, he could not stand up in the cramped space. Tate was ordered by Lord Salisbury to starve the priest out, if necessary. Although she was watched very closely, Elizabeth still managed to get food and water to Gerard and, in the last days of the search, she was even able to free him long enough to stretch his legs and warm himself by the fire.

The priest search lasted for two days and revealed nothing. Tate was tempted to call the siege off because of the family's seemingly innocent responses to his questioning. That is, until another priest was captured. His name was Thomas Laithwaite and he had also been staying at Harrowden Hall. His capturer took him to an inn, intending to examine him, and commit him the next day. Laithwaite laid his cloak and sword on the bench and, on the pretence of leading his horse to the stream so that it might drink, he told the lad to go back to the stable and get some hay, saying he would bring the animal back shortly. The lad, not suspecting anything, did as he was told. The priest mounted his horse and rode off, later taking shelter in a friend's house for the night. Having laid low he then started on his journey again, thinking that the danger was past, and rode straight back into Tate's cordon around Harrowden Hall. After this event, Tate resumed his search with renewed vigour on Thursday 14th November. Day after day the Protestants ransacked the house, until Lady Vaux, in the hope of distracting the searchers, allowed her manservant, Richard Richardson, to reveal the secret room behind some panelling. All that was found were some popish books and pamphlets. Tate was to say later that it was the most secret room that he had ever seen. Little did he know that only a wall's thickness away the man that he was seeking was hiding, stooped and hardly daring to breathe. After several more days of surveillance, Tate was convinced that there was no priest hiding in the house.

Once more Lord Salisbury sent instructions to William Tate. This time he was to arrest Elizabeth Vaux and bring her to London. On Saturday, 16th November Lady Vaux and her son Edward accompanied Tate and his companions on an uncomfortable journey to the capital. Elizabeth was examined by Salisbury and a group of commissioners. She was never brought to trial and was released on bond to Mr Lewis Pickering, on condition she remained in London. Eventually, Lady Vaux was allowed to return to Harrowden Hall to resume the sort of life she had led before.

As for the other characters in the drama, after the relentless search of Harrowden Hall had finally ended Father Gerard escaped to another county and a year later went to Rome.

Nicholas Owen, however, who had built the ingenious priest hole that had outwitted Tate and 100 determined soldiers, was not so lucky. It was ironic, after 26 years of travelling about the countryside constructing hiding holes in the homes of Catholic gentry, which had saved the lives of hundreds of priests, that he should be caught himself. Often working alone, he shared the secret of the hiding places only with the owner of the house. Owen was finally captured at Hindlip Castle, near Worcester. He was horribly tortured and died in prison.

The present Harrowden Hall was built around 1719, on the foundations of the dilapidated Vaux manor house. It is a plain, square house, set behind splendid wrought iron gates and, with well-tended gardens, is now the clubhouse of the Wellingborough Golf Club.

5

The Landowner and the Parson

FOR hundreds of years the hamlet of Grafton Underwood, just north of Kettering, was part of the Boughton estate and generations of the inhabitants worked for the Montagu family, who lived at Boughton House nearby. Sir Edward Montagu, Chief Justice of the King's Bench, purchased Boughton House in 1528. His son, Edward, was known as a great 'friend' of Kettering, because of the great interest he took in the town. But it was Ralph, the first Duke of Montagu, who rebuilt Boughton House in 1683 in the grand style of a French chateau. It is now the home of the Duke of Buccleuch and one of the great houses of the county.

In 1602 the grandson of the Chief Justice (yet another Sir Edward), inherited the estate, at the age of 40, and became the first Baron Montagu. He was a strict Puritan and highly respected by his neighbours, but in 1618 he became engaged in a bitter quarrel with the Rector of Grafton Underwood.

The village feast was to be celebrated that year on Saturday, 25th July, St James' Day, the parish church's patronal festival, but the merry-making often went on for more than one day. The austere landowner, however, determined to restrict the scope of the activities. Sir Edward and Sir Thomas Brookes of Great Oakley were Justices of the Peace, and it was in that capacity that they issued a warrant to the constable of Grafton. The warrant contained certain clauses – firstly that it was forbidden to sell unlicensed beer (ale brewed in the cottages) at the annual feast fair, secondly that no games or exercises should take place on the Sabbath, thirdly that any fiddlers coming to Grafton of their own accord, and not at the request of the local people, should be treated as rogues and put in the stocks, and lastly that any persons visiting the feast from other places should be asked to leave.

News of the warrant came to the notice of the Welsh parson of the village. Dr John Williams, who was in his parsonage at Grafton, demanded that the constable should show him the warrant, which he refused to do, but the parson threatened to 'lay him by the heels' if he did not. It was soon delivered into his hands.

Dr Williams read the warrant out publicly in the churchyard before the evening service, and promptly cancelled the clauses of the document. He pronounced that he was a 'Justice of the Peace, Quorum, Doctor and Parson of the village', and that the alewives should sell their liquor, that any fiddlers coming to Grafton should play, that any games or exercises not prohibited by the law should take place and also that any strangers from other villages coming to Grafton on the feast day should be allowed to stay. To the great joy of the inhabitants of Grafton, their parson won the day for them and the feast went ahead without curtailment.

Edward Montagu was most displeased at having his authority flouted by the parson and set about trying to make an example of Dr Williams. He approached Sir Henry Hobart, the Chief Justice of the Common Pleas, but found to his disappointment that he was cool towards him and paid little attention to the matter of the dispute. Then Sir Edward tried to get his brother, Sir Henry Montagu, to speak to the King, on his behalf, concerning the difference of opinion. He wrote to Henry on 5th December 1618, beseeching him to 'stir in it, either by acquainting his Majesty or any course according to your wisdom.' Unfortunately for Sir Edward, sympathy in high places was on the side of Dr Williams, for it seems nothing was done, and there the business had to rest.

The Rector had not been afraid to stand up to a powerful member of the nobility for he had the backing of some very influential people. He owed his position of Justice of the Peace to no less a person than Francis Bacon, Lord Chancellor, and had been brought to the notice of King James I by James Montagu, Bishop of Winchester, Sir Edward's brother. The King made Williams his chaplain, and presented him to the living of Grafton Underwood in 1611. Three years later he also became the Rector of Walgrave, where he mostly resided. He was an energetic and conscientious clergyman, for he preached twice every Sunday at either Walgrave or Grafton and read the liturgy on Wednesdays and Fridays, also enjoying the pursuits of music and gardening.

In 1619, a year after the affair of Grafton's feast day, Dr Williams became the Dean of Salisbury, so it seemed that, in spite of Sir Edward's efforts to restrain the parson, it didn't have any harmful effect on his career. He went on to become the Bishop of Lincoln and, subequently, the Archbishop of York.

6

Rockingham Castle – Garrison of the Roundheads

THE ancient castle of Rockingham, standing on a steep
hillside overlooking the lovely Welland valley, has seen
many reversals of fortune over the years and, if a building
could be said to have any, its loyalties must certainly be
divided.

It was originally a strong keep built by William the
Conqueror, in the midst of the immense forest which stretched
over much of Northamptonshire, and stayed in by him when
hunting. It was subsequently used by the early kings of
England as a centre from which both to administer the
Midlands and to chase the red deer in the forest. During
medieval times, many important events took place there, such
as one of the earliest recorded assemblies of state, when in
1095 a number of nobles, bishops and clergy were summoned
by William Rufus to settle a dispute between himself and
Anselm, the Archbishop of Canterbury. In 1217, the Earl of
Albermarle, constable of the castle, rebelled against the young
Henry III. Three years later the King sent Fawkes de Breauté
to lay siege to Rockingham Castle at the suggestion of his
mother, Queen Isabella, and was subsequently brought to
watch the fighting. The garrison ran out of food, and the Earl
eventually surrendered.

By the 15th century, Rockingham Castle had become derelict and a hunting lodge was built in the park for Henry VII to stay in whilst hunting.

In 1530, Edward Watson obtained a lease on the royal castle and grounds, from Henry VIII. By now the building was little more than a ruin, so Edward moved into the hunting lodge with his family and spent the rest of his life repairing what remained of the Norman castle and turning it into a comfortable Tudor dwelling.

Edward Watson stood in high esteem with James I, who knighted his son, another Edward, in 1603. He carried on his father's good work on the castle and was a competent administrator of the land. It was his son, Sir Lewis Watson, who purchased the freehold of the Rockingham estate for a 'considerable sum'. However, the King reserved the right to hunt in the forest and came to stay at the castle as a guest of Sir Lewis on the 29th July 1619. He was the last king to visit Rockingham.

Sir Lewis set about improving the pleasure grounds, and obtained royal sanction to divert the high road further east. His first wife, Catherine Bertie, died in childbirth, and ten years later, in 1620, he married for the second time. This was to Eleanor Manners, daughter of Sir George Manners of Hadden in Derbyshire, and sister of John, the 8th Earl of Rutland. Theirs was a happy union and they produced six daughters and one surviving son. Sir Lewis was related by kinship and marriage to many of the leading families in the district. In 1634, he was High Sheriff of the county and highly respected by his neighbours. Around this time, he increased his properties by purchasing the 'fairs, markets and bakehouse' of Kettering. A year later he acquired Hunters Manor in Little Weldon, which made him Master of The Royal Buckhounds, a hereditary post. In 1638 he also bought the manors of Stoke Albany and Wilbarston.

For all his wealth and properties, Lewis was essentially a peaceful, home-loving man and did not want to get involved with politics. But this was the start of a very troubled era, when a serious rift was widening between the King and Parliament. His family were divided in their loyalties, as was the case with many families at that time. He was a Royalist, but his wife's brother supported Parliament. Sir Lewis expected Rockingham to be taken as a Royalist garrison and so, to insure against all eventualities, decided to send his plate and valuables into safe-keeping at Belvoir Castle, which at that time was a Parliamentary stronghold. This action proved to be the wrong one, as Belvoir was taken by the Royalists and Rockingham by the Roundheads. So, unfortunately, Sir Lewis lost everything.

Lord Grey, of Groby, was made Sergeant Major General and raised 8,000 men in Northamptonshire and the surrounding counties for the Parliamentarian cause. He arrived suddenly at Rockingham on the 19th March 1643 and took possession of the castle. Sir Lewis and his family were conveyed to his brother's house at Stoke Park, further up the Welland valley at Stoke Albany.

Colonel Hastings, a Royalist leader, swept through the county with his troops, and came to the Rockingham neighbourhood via Wellingborough and Kettering, reaching Stoke Park by May. He pounced on Sir Lewis and his brother, Sir Edward, and made them his prisoners, on the charge that no real attempt had been made to hold Rockingham Castle for the King. They were then sent to Belvoir Castle. After a short period they were moved to Ashby de la Zouch, for greater security. The Watsons were detained at Ashby until the August of 1643 and then, in response to Sir Lewis' frequent petitions, he and his brother were sent to Oxford, where he waited to see the King and clear himself of the charges of disloyalty that had been brought against him.

33

Meanwhile, back at Rockingham Castle, Lord Grey fortified the building strongly. He then left Sir John Norwich of Brampton Ash in command as his services were needed elsewhere. It must have been particularly galling for Sir Lewis when he heard this news, as Norwich was the grandson of his sister, Anne. Eleanor and their children were still at Stoke Park and she wrote often to her husband and must have kept him informed of what was happening at Rockingham.

The Royalists tried to take the castle on many occasions but were always unsuccessful. There is a traditional tale connected with the time that Rockingham was occupied by the Roundheads, that one particular night the sentinels inside the castle walls heard strange noises coming from the grounds. They were alarmed that the sounds indicated that a body of Royalist troops was approaching the castle in order to besiege the fortress. They challenged the attackers and, having got no reply, fired upon them. This aroused the garrison who rushed to their aid and resulted in a continuous discharge of firearms. Still the party of besiegers didn't return their fire and even more unearthly sounds were heard. This only served to frighten the Roundheads even more and the idea was put about that some devilish practices were afoot. Not having the courage to go out and see what was going on in the darkness, they waited until daylight, when the embarrassing truth was revealed to them. What they had imagined to be a besieging party of Royalists, or, worse still, a supernatural being, was in fact nothing more than a herd of squealing swine that had strayed into the grounds from the nearby forest.

During the time the Roundheads were stationed at Rockingham, great damage was caused to the castle and surrounding area. Sir John Norwich ordered that the almshouses should be pulled down, as well as the building for imprisoning the poachers, eleven cottages and most of the church. This was done because the Parliamentarians feared that these buildings might be used by the opposing parties for shelter.

Sir Lewis Watson was eventually granted a pardon and released from prison. He was present at the final council of Oxford and was created Lord Rockingham by the King.

The Roundheads demolished the great keep and the curtain walls, before handing Lord Rockingham back his property. His splendid Tudor house had been stripped of its contents and his pleasure grounds destroyed. Lewis never really recovered from his experiences in the Civil War and became an embittered man. He spent what was left of his life trying to repair the damage to his beloved castle and seeking restitution from the Government for his losses. He died in 1652, aged 68, and was succeeded by his son Edward, 2nd Lord Rockingham. His wife Eleanor survived her husband by 26 years, and lived mostly at her Dower House at Great Easton.

The bustling market town of Rockingham, which had 1,800 inhabitants in the reign of Queen Elizabeth, contracted after the Civil War into the small village that exists today, its castle now a pleasing mixture of architectural styles, a wealth of stories secreted within its walls.

7

John Maidwell, Dissenter

IN the mid 17th century, Kettering was just a small town, roughly the size of Burton Latimer to the south. The houses were built of stone with thatched roofs, and the only buildings of any note were the parish church and the manor house. It was, however, a well-known centre for Puritanism.

This was a hard age to live in, especially if your religious beliefs differed from the tenets of the established church, and it was also the time of the Great Plague. By 1665 between 70 and 80 people had died in Kettering, with 'PL' marked next to their names in the burial register.

One particular evening, several people were hurrying along the main street towards the Market Square. It was dark and they carefully stepped over the rubbish in the gutters, the footpaths being unpaved. When they came to the White Hart (renamed the Royal Hotel in 1844, to commemorate a visit of Queen Victoria), they turned into Hazelwood Lane. The men looked serious and were solemnly dressed. The women seemed frightened and talked to one another in whispers. Their destination was Hazelwood House, where they were going to attend an illegal meeting. The Dissenters, for such they were, quietly entered the building, and the door was locked and bolted. A guard was placed at the entrance and one further up the street, to give a warning of any constable or an informer who might give them away. Then the candles were lit and the bible was taken out of its hiding place. A prayer was said by one of the elders, but the small congregation dared not sing a hymn in case it was overheard. Afterwards, a chapter was read from the bible. Then, at last, came the moment they had been waiting for, when a letter was read out aloud, sent to them by their beloved absent pastor, the Reverend John Maidwell. He was in hiding at Marston Trussell, a village twelve miles away.

John Maidwell was born at Geddington around the year 1609 and he was Rector of Kettering from 1651 until 1662. In that year he relinquished his living, because, as a Puritan, his conscience would not allow him to accept on oath the Book of Common Prayer as the only legal service book. Parliament was seeking to impose religious uniformity throughout the country by restoring the overall authority of the Church of England after the return of the monarchy, and the clergy were given until the 24th August, St Bartholomew's Day, to accept the new law. John Maidwell was one of the 46 clergymen in Northamptonshire who refused and so had to leave the established church.

In the early days of the changes, the Reverend Maidwell suffered from much persecution, especially from the younger brother of Edmund Sawyer, the Lord of the Manor (who built the almshouses at the top of what is now Station Road). Sometimes Maidwell only escaped from Sawyer by disguising himself, but on one occasion it was said that the parson had to spend a short spell in gaol. He survived the ordeal and was allowed under the Indulgence Act to preach at 'Widow Cooper's' house, but continued to hold meetings in his own house and others. Hazelwood House, which could still be seen up to 1955, when it was demolished, was a favourite venue for the Dissenters' gatherings (it belonged to his grand-daughter, Mrs Hazelwood), because it had an easy access for a quick escape from the premises. At the back of the second storey, there was a small window from where a fugitive could get out onto an adjoining roof and thence climb down to ground level.

Tradition has it that on several occasions when the meeting of Puritans was in progress, a knock would come at the door, which would give a warning of the soldiers. Before they could make a forced entry, Maidwell and the more agile of his companions would make a quick getaway from the little upstairs window and they would be on their way across the fields towards Rothwell.

Then came two Acts of Parliament which changed matters drastically for the nonconformists. The first one was the Conventicle Act, which prohibited gatherings of more than five people meeting for worship other than at Church of England services. The second was the Five Mile Act, which forbade dissenting ministers to live within five miles of any corporate town, or of where they had formerly preached.

John Maidwell had to leave Kettering and go and live in secret at Marston Trussel. It was from there that he wrote several 'Pastoral Letters' to his followers in Kettering.

However, the nonconformists had their own place of worship in the town some years before the Toleration Act was passed in 1689. The first congregational church was situated in Allen's Yard, at the back of the present Midland Bank. It was constructed partly of brick and stone with a thatched roof, and had a gallery inside. The building measured 48 ft long by 40 ft wide and was capable of holding a congregation of 300 to 400 people. The Reverend John Maidwell continued in his ministry almost to his death in 1692, when he was 83, and he was buried in the chancel of Kettering parish church.

8

The Notorious Parson of Wappenham

WE will probably never know why Theophilus Hart was appointed Rector of Wappenham – he was not even in holy orders, and was a rogue into the bargain.

He received the living from Robert Wallop, Lord of the Manor, who dispossessed the Reverend Caesar Williamson in 1642. Wallop was a staunch Parlimentarian, being one of the lawyers who sat in judgement on Charles I and supervised the execution of the King in 1649. He was later to be imprisoned for this and he died in the Tower.

In 1650, as his fortune declined, he gave instructions to his bailiff, Mr Reeve, and Mr Hart to sell his property in the village. Most of it, however, ended up in the hands of Hart by sharp practice, at a price agreed to be 'very cheap'. The parson's buy included the 'Lordship of the Manor' and the tithes and glebe lands belonging to the rectory. He made good use of his title and brought many lawsuits against the parishioners, for the purpose of encroaching on their property.

After the restoration of Charles II he managed to hold onto the position of Rector by applying to the Bishop of Peterborough (it should have been the Bishop of Lincoln). He passed the necessary examination for holy orders by bribing the Bishop's secretary with £5 and a brace of bucks. Hart had a curate to read the services for him and dig the garden, in return for his board and £5 a year.

The wicked parson continued to enjoy his ill gotten gains until 23rd January 1685, when George Tarry, a local butcher got his revenge. Hart was thought to be having an affair with his wife. Tarry is supposed to have chased him over hedges, ditches and stiles on many occasions in the past without catching him, although the amorous parson was at least 65 at the time. The butcher decided on this particular day in January that he had put up with enough and took an axe to the rectory. He forced open the bedroom door and saw what he had long suspected. His wife was lying stark-naked in bed with the parson. Tarry was now beside himself with jealousy and anger and leapt onto the bed. Before Hart could defend himself his head was cleaved open with the butcher's axe.

Hart's children, Rachel, Anne and Martha, were joint heiresses to his estate. Rachel, however, seems to have inherited some of her father's bad traits for, after many lawsuits, she and her husband, Reverend Timothy Hart of Blakesley, (who, by sheer coincidence, shared the same surname as Rachel's family name) ended up as the sole possessors.

9

'It Fastens the Teeth...'

A DESCRIPTION of the once famous spa at Astrop was given by Dr Thomas Short MD of Sheffield in 1734, when it was in its heyday:

'The water springs up from the well into a close strong basin and empties itself by a long neat gutter, cut out of freestone, with the wellhead there is a house with pallisadoes before it, from this the company go under a shelter into another very large sashed, wainscoted, boarded room, where they can walk, drink coffee or tea, and in the afternoon meet, converse. Behind this is a noble, dry, fine gravel walk, 140 yards long, 6 ft broad, with charming clipped close set hedge 12 ft high, with several neat benches on each side, at the farther end of which, are conveniences for the drinkers to retire when their water operates.

'On the other side of the brook from the well is a fine tea room, dancing room and a kitchen etc and nearby there is a convenient shop.'

The spring was discovered by Dr Richard Lower in 1664. He and his companion, a Dr Willis, were travelling through the neighbourhood on horseback to visit some patients. The physician saw that the stones in the stream were discoloured and thought that this might be an indication of iron. He put some powder in the water, which immediately turned a blackish colour. He promptly declared that in the future he wouldn't send his patients as far as Tunbridge but to Astrop instead.

The doctors from Oxbridge said that the chalybeate spring had medicinal properties and called it after St Rumbold, the 7th century baby saint, said to have been born at Walton Fields near Kings Sutton. Thus Astrop Spa came into being. In 1688 a 'learned physician' made fantastic claims about the properties of the Astrop waters in a pamphlet (shades of modern TV advertising):

'It penetrates every occult passage where other medicines cannot come, it fastens the teeth though ready to drop out, takes away old and long continued headache, vertigo, palsey and all sorts of gout.'

Many wealthy and influential people came to visit the spring, among them Horace Walpole. We read that it was patronised by the North family of Wroxton. Mr and Mrs Brudenell went there in 1739, and Thomas Thornton of Brockhall in 1740. Mr Thornton was very taken with the place and he and his family stayed there year after year. Two royal visitors were the Prince and Princess of Wales (the parents of George III). They partook of a breakfast there before going on to visit the Cartwrights in Aynho. At the height of its popularity, Astrop Spa could boast of weekly balls on Mondays and cards and dancing during the season.

In 1749 a new well was opened at King's Sutton, half a mile away from the old one, with great solemnity. A breakfast was provided by Anthony Keck of Leicestershire in gratitude for the benefit he had received. But, sadly, by the late 1770s the little spa had declined, and the lodging houses had become run down, other great spas, such as Leamington and Bath, having become much more fashionable places to visit. Up until about 1808 the 'Great Room' was still opened at Astrop every year in June and July, for entertainments for the public, but after this time the buildings were left to crumble away.

Gone are the great assembly hall, the gravel walk, the hedge, seats, tea room and shop. All that is left now is the ornamental wellhead of St Rumbold, which stands in a hollow in the grounds of Astrop House, and a replica wellhead, known as Astrop well, situated on the side of the Charlton road. A very different scene from the bustle depicted by Dr Short.

10

'The Order of the White Collar'

'VIEW halloo!' The cry has been a familiar sound in Northamptonshire for a very long time, the county's connection with hunting dating back even to Roman times. Later, the kings of England had their royal hunting lodges in the immense forests around Whittlebury and Rockingham.

The tiny village of Pytchley traces its hunting tradition back to Saxon times, when Penda, the King of Mercia (577-655) hunted in the vicinity. Then, some 800 years later, in the reign of Richard III, the lords of the manor of Pytchley were bound by a service to the Crown, whereby they had to keep hunting dogs to kill the wolves, foxes, polecats and other vermin in Northamptonshire, Oxfordshire, Buckinghamshire and Essex. This obligation continued until the time of Charles II.

When foxhunting became widely popular in the 18th century, the superb grasslands of Northamptonshire offered some of the best country available for this type of field sport, and, round about 1750, John George, Earl Spencer, formed a Hunt Club at Pytchley Hall and built kennels there for his hounds. The Hall was a large Elizabethan mansion built by Euseby Isham. It was situated across the present Isham Street, facing west to the church.

The Pytchley Hunt Club was very exclusive, the membership being by invitation only and limited to 40. The hard-riding huntsmen had the right to stay at the Hall in

temporary accommodation for as long as it suited them, and were able to stable their horses. The building was lent to the hunt, for which they didn't have to pay any rent, for as long as they kept it in good repair and paid the taxes. It must have been a very large house as it could accommodate as many as 20 members and their servants at any one time. We are told that in 1775 the extensive stables gave work to twelve grooms, four men who looked after the hacks, two coachmen and four postilions, with five other men being employed in the kennels.

Members of the club were known as 'The Order of the White Collar', and the following names of titled nobility who were on the list give some indication of how fashionable and popular it was – the Earl of Jersey, the Earl of Westmoreland, the Marquis of Graham, Viscount Althorp, Duke of Devonshire, Viscount Torrington, the Earl of Winchelsea and Lord Cavendish, to name just a few.

In 1765 Lord Spencer introduced the system of dividing up the county into two parts, the woodlands and open countryside east of Northampton and the Market Harborough road being hunted in one part of the year, and the land west of the dividing line in the other. The hunt was thereafter called the Althorp and Pytchley.

In about 1777, a remarkable huntsman, Dick Knight, took over from the previous huntsman, a Mr Knight (no relation), who had to retire due to a bad fall. Dick was born at Courteenhall on the 2nd January 1742. He joined the Althorp stables, and had an amazing voice which could be heard over a long distance. It was said that on a clear, frosty morning, his call of 'Halloo' in Sywell Wood could be heard in Wellingborough, three miles away as the crow flies.

The Pytchley Hunt at that time adjoined, at its northern boundary, the Quorn Hunt country in Leicestershire, and there was said to be a lot of jealous rivalry between the two hunts. On one occasion a Mr Assheton Smith had come over

47

to the Pytchley Hunt with the sole purpose of 'culling down' the celebrated huntsman, Dick Knight. He approached Dick, and said that he had heard a great deal about his riding skills, and wagered him the horse he was riding if he could beat him on that day. Knight agreed to the bet and, during the run, the riders came to a fence which could only be jumped by passing underneath a tree that had branches hanging down. There was scarcely any room for a horse and rider to get through. Knight was not to be daunted and, lying down flat on his horse's back, he threw his legs around its neck and passed through the narrow space with ease. Assheton Smith did not want to take a similar risk and did not follow, but he did the honourable thing and sent his best hunter, Egmont, over to the daring horseman the next day.

Dick Knight retired to a farm at Thrapston and, when he died in 1806, was buried in Brigstock churchyard.

Earl Spencer died at the comparatively early age of 49, in 1783, and his son, another John George, took over as Master of the Hunt when he was 25. He held the office for 15 years until he had to relinquish it due to his political duties.

The elegant old Pytchley Hall passed into the hands of George Payne, a Regency buck, who was for some time Master of the Pytchley. Payne was one of the greatest gamblers in English 'Society'. His father had been killed in a duel and George inherited £300,000, which he ran through in no time. In one year alone he lost £33,000 and in 1829, due to his gambling losses, the Pytchley house had to be pulled down, and Sulby Hall, the original family home of the Paynes, had to be sold to pay his debts.

The Pytchely Hunt Club continued until 1819, when Sir Charles Knightley and several other gentleman decided to move the hounds to new kennels, more in the centre of the county. By now the old system of dividing the hunting area into two halves had been abandoned and the old club was closed. It marked the end of an era. From this time the hunt became known as the Pytchley, but the ancient link with hunting in the village of Pytchley itself was broken for ever.

11

An Unusual Request

THE village of Whilton was once the scene of one of the most bizarre burials, or, rather, non-burials, on record.

The Reverend Freeman Langton was born in 1710, and he later became the Rector of Bilton in Warwickshire and the Lord of the Manor of Whilton. He never married and he became a very eccentric character, as his will, which he made at the age of 73, certainly indicates.

An extract from the document, which was dated 16th of September 1783, gives some very weird instructions as to his burial:

'. . . and first, for four or five days after my decease, and until by body grows offensive, I would not be removed out of the place or bed I shall die on, and then I would be carried and laid in the same bed, decently and privately, in the summer house now erected in the garden belonging to the dwelling house where I now inhabit in Whilton, and to be laid in the same bed there, with all the apputtenances thereto belonging, and to be wrapped in a strong double winding sheet, and in all other respects to be interred as near as may be to the description we receive in Holy Scripture of our Saviour's burial, the doors and windows to be bolted, and to be kept as near in the same manner and state they shall be at the time of my decease and I desire that the building or summer house may be planted round with evergreen plants, and fenced off with iron or oak pales and painted a dark blue colour.'

The Reverend Freeman Langton died a year later on the 9th October 1784. His strange behests were carried out in the appropriate manner two days later, and his corpse was enveloped in his feather bed in the summer house.

The Rector left the manor of Whilton, together with his house and lands, to his nephew, Thomas Freeman of Daventry.

In the 19th century, an entrance was made through the roof of the summer house and the body was seen to be still intact. By the early 1970s, however, when the manor house stood empty for a time, all that was left of the Rector's summer house was a stone arch covered with ivy. The new owners demolished this surviving part of the building because it had become unsafe. No trace was found of the Reverend Langton's body.

Perhaps it had been interred in the churchyard, but there is no record of this and the whereabouts of the eccentric churchman's earthly remains continues to be a mystery.

12

A Notable Prize Fight – And a Notable Fighter

PRIZE fighting was peculiarly an English sport and flourished in the years between 1750-1850. The pugilists became national heroes and fought with their bare hands, in long, punishing combat which often lasted for 70 rounds or more and only ended when one of them could no longer stand. Their injuries were terrible and sometimes fatal. The sport became a favourite preoccupation of all classes of society, although the fighters themselves, and most of the spectators, came from the working class. Prize fighting was a violent activity in a brutal age and the contests attracted huge crowds, sometimes in their tens of thousands, even though such matches were illegal.

Before Jack Broughton, himself a former fighter, thought up a set of rules for boxing at his amphitheatre in London in 1743, meetings between the pugilists had been degrading and without any semblance of decency or order. Broughton introduced the idea of boxers using gloves, called mufflers. His rules lasted almost unchanged for the next hundred years.

In 1814 the Pugilist Club was formed by several parties of prize fighters. The leading boxers were backed financially by their patrons, who put up the purse for which the opponents contended at the fight. The parties also backed their own nominee, whether he won or lost, and supported him when he was in training. A boxer did not always receive the sum of money staked in his name, but he was entitled to half the gate money.

The fights usually took place on a grass surface in a ring most commonly formed with ropes and stakes. In the middle was a mark or scratch and the boxers had to come up to this (the origin of the phrase 'up to the mark') at the beginning of the fight and at the end of each half minute break. The contests took place in all seasons, whatever the weather and occasionally in wild, remote places.

One such place was Sutfield Green at the extreme end of Whittlebury Forest, near to the boundary line of Buckinghamshire. It was a favourite venue for prize fights in the 18th and 19th centuries. This out-of-the-way, wooded area offered a safe and secluded spot in which the fights could be held, for it was possible, if the authorities got to hear of the illegal match, for the lawbreakers to slip over the border into the next county, where the constable could not follow them.

One notable fight took place there on the 9th September 1845, between William (Bendigo) Thompson and Ben Caunt for the championship of England. The contest was at first arranged to take place in Newport Pagnell, and Bendigo and his backers had put up at the Swan. His fans had arrived at Newport by canal and they looted the bakers' shops in the town. They were sarcastically nicknamed 'the lambs' because of their reputation of being the most unruly crowd in the country. A warrant was issued against the boxer and his promoters, but Bendigo managed to go into hiding at a local farmhouse.

In the meantime, his opponent, Caunt, had taken shelter at the Cock at Stony Stratford. The sudden decision by the authorities that the fight must not take place in Buckinghamshire put the arrangements for the proposed match into disarray. New plans were drawn up and they chose Whaddon as the meeting place. As there was nothing they could do about it, the fans started off on the ten mile trek to Whaddon where the ring had been set up, but, to the consternation of the promoters, they were informed that the new venue was still in Buckinghamshire. Once more the loyal fans, who must by now have been very disappointed, set off, this time for Sutfield Green, a further eight miles.

Some 10,000 people gathered at the edge of the forest to watch Bendigo and Caunt fight for the championship. Before the contest could start, there was an argument as to who should be the referee. Squire Osbaldeston was sitting in his carriage waiting for the match to begin, when he was approached and asked if he would perform the duties of referee. The famous squire, a devout follower of the sport, and a former master of the Pytchley Hunt, reluctantly agreed to officiate at the proceedings.

The fight took place under the London Price Ring Rules of 1838, which stated that there had to be two accomplices and a referee, who was expected to settle all disputes. Each round would last until one or both boxers went down. Then the seconds, who up to this point would not have been allowed into the ring, would enter it, lead the men to their particular corners and try to revive them. The referee would call time after 30 seconds and each boxer would have to walk unaided to the mark in the middle of the ring. The participant who failed to 'come up to scratch' was said to be the loser.

It would be quite possible for the contest to go on for hours.

When at last the Bendigo/Caunt fight got underway, a terrific battle took place, and lasted for 93 rounds! In the 92nd the supporters of Caunt claimed that Bendigo had struck his opponent a foul blow and the umpires, who were unable to agree, appealed to the referee for his opinion. The Squire said he had not seen anything and the match continued. The next and final round saw Caunt fall without a blow from Bendigo. This time Squire Osbaldeston saw what happened and awarded victory to Bendigo. For, according to the new laws, any boxer falling without receiving a blow was adjudged to have lost the fight.

The Squire had tackled an unenviable task when asked to take over as referee at that particular boxing match, for both pugilists had been guilty at previous contests of fighting unfairly. In their last two fights Bendigo and Caunt had gained unsatisfactory victories by the means of a foul. Also, Bendigo was well known for his devious boxing technique.

Caunt thought he had won so, when the verdict was given stating otherwise, ructions broke out, and his supporters turned on Bendigo's fans and a punch-up followed. Having given way to their pent-up energies and frustrations, the exhausted spectators streamed back to Stony Stratford and drank every pub in the town dry – some landlords were even reduced to serving water!

Caunt subsequently retired from the ring, but Bendigo fought once more for the championship, which he again won on a dubious verdict. Back in his home town of Nottingham he was something of a legend. Born in the slums, he was one of triplets, in a huge family of 21 children. After he had finished with the ring, he started drinking heavily and was always in trouble with the police, spending many days in gaol. At the age of 60, however, he was converted by a preacher, Richard Weaver, and became an evangelical preacher himself. The old pugilist had his own way of dealing with any troublemakers who came to mock him at his change of heart. For on one occasion several boxers turned up to annoy him at the Ebenezer chapel where he was speaking. He laid down his bible, and knocked them flat with his huge fists.

Bendigo died in 1880 and thousands of people followed his funeral cortège.

13

An Industrious Man

JOHN Cole was a remarkable man, although by worldly standards he could be said to have been a total failure.

Born at Weston Favell in 1792, he grew up and went to Northampton to be an apprentice to W. Birdsall, a bookseller. Whilst there he wrote his first book, at the age of 23, *A History of Northampton and its Vicinity*. This was to be the first of many books by him on local history at a time when the life of the 'common man' was not considered to be interesting enough to be properly recorded. It was published in 1815.

Two years later he married Susanna Marshall of Northampton and then moved to Lincoln, where he bought a business for £1,000 and set up as a bookseller himself. The venture turned out to be a financial disaster. Unfortunately, this failure was to set the pattern for his future life. For although he was a man of letters he did not have any business acumen. From Lincoln he moved to Hull, then to Scarborough. Whilst at Lincoln and Scarborough he wrote the histories of the towns. At all these places his businesses collapsed and he was ruined. Although he had worked like a demon and had written many books, they did not generate sufficient income. As well as his writings, he also gave lectures on astronomy, architecture and natural history, and was said to be a good speaker, but all this effort brought him very little financial reward.

He sank into debt and returned to Northampton, where he opened a shop on the market square. John lectured in the town on natural history and philosophy, but all to no avail. He was still not making enough money to keep himself solvent and once more he had to close down his business. His wife died in 1832 and he went to live in Wellingborough, where he opened a small school. He had a little shop in his front room and supplemented his meagre income by selling fossils, apples, bacon and ham – and he still found time to write a history of that town, too. He delighted in taking his pupils out into the countryside, where they would collect many specimens. He was, however, thought to be peculiar because he did such a thing.

Cole's school in Wellingborough failed and he eventually went to live in Woodford, in 1845, where he spent his remaining years. Once more he tried his hand at teaching, in a house in Club Lane. He called this 'The Academy'. The building is now Priory Cottage and is joined to what used to be the Working Men's Club. He wrote a history of Woodford in the brief time he had left, dying of starvation and in abject poverty in 1848, aged 56. He was buried in an unmarked grave.

John Cole produced over 100 books, including histories of Ecton, Irthlingborough and Higham Ferrers. He also wrote on other subjects, such as religion, biography and literature. Natural history was his first love, however, and his references to plants and flowers are very accurate. He will be best remembered for his careful writing about the villages and towns of Northampton and, although he was untrained, his observations are still of interest to local historians and to anyone who wants to delve into the past.

What a pity his talents were not recognised in his lifetime!

14

Adeline, Countess of Cardigan

ADELINE de Horsey was born on Christmas Eve in 1824, the daughter of Spencer de Horsey and Lady Louisa de Horsey. Her parents moved in fashionable circles, and when she was 17 Adeline was presented at court. By this time she had blossomed into a lovely young woman with dark hair and a good figure. Three years later she attended a fancy dress ball at which the handsome and dashing James Thomas Brudenell, 7th Earl of Cardigan, appeared as an 18th-century dragoon. Soon afterwards, Adeline and her mother visited Deene Hall, the country estate of Lord Cardigan. When her mother died a year later, Miss de Horsey took over her role as hostess in her father's house.

It was some years before Lord Cardigan and Adeline met again, but then they fell seriously in love. The fact that he was 60, and 27 years older than her, did not seem to make any difference. The real problem was that Cardigan's wife was still alive. Their affair began to scandalise London society, and Adeline was forbidden by her father from seeing Lord Cardigan again. The infatuated socialite defied him and devised an ingenious method of communicating with her admirer. She would let down a piece of string, weighted with a piece of coal, at the time Cardigan rode past on his way to the park. He would stop and tie a note to the lump of coal and Miss de Horsey would pull up the missive. In the end, matters

59

were brought to a head when Adeline had a blazing row with her father and walked out. She and Cardigan set up house in Norfolk Street, just off Park Lane, where they lived openly together for some years.

In 1858 the Earl's wife died and the lovers were free to marry, which they did three months later by special licence in the garrison chapel on the Rock of Gibraltar. After a long honeymoon they returned to England and went to take up married life in Northamptonshire at Deene Hall. Their life together was a happy one despite their difference in age, and the fact that they were ostracised by the nobility. They entertained a lot at Deene and in London. Both of them rode to hounds with the Pytchley and the Quorn, and Lord Cardigan was still invited to various functions at Buckingham Palace, even though the Queen disapproved of him. This period was, for the Earl, probably the most contented of his turbulent life.

In the spring of 1868, after 10 years of marriage, Lord Cardigan complained of feeling giddy whilst out riding. A few days later he went out again with his wife and a guest. A groom came up with the news that one of the gamekeepers had accidently been shot dead. Cardigan rode off to the scene of the incident and, afterwards, when he had commiserated with the dead man's relatives, he set off for home. When he was only a quarter of a mile from the Hall, he fell from his horse. A road surveyor found him and helped Lord Cardigan to his feet, shouting to some women in their cottage gardens to come and give him a hand. They supported the Earl along the road until they were met by the carriage. The Earl never recovered from his fall and died two days later, on the 28th March, aged 71 years.

The funeral was spectacular, as befitted a national hero. The coffin was covered with crimson velvet, and four officers of the 11th Hussars acted as pall bearers. Lord Cardigan's valet, Mr Matthews, led the procession, holding the Earl's coronet on a crimson cushion in his outstretched arms. His favourite charger, Ronald, which he had ridden at Balaclava, as leader of the Light Brigade, was led by the grooms behind the coffin. The family mourners followed immediately after, wearing their high chimney pot hats. Then came 62 farm tenants from the various estates, and, bringing up the rear, the bandsmen from Cardigan's private band and the keepers in their green liveries. The cortège made its slow and impressive way into the church at Deene, which was packed with friends and villagers from Deene and Deenethorpe.

Adeline, however, had a lot of living still to do.

Just after the funeral, one of the relatives of the heir to his estates was pacing up and down on the south terrace at Deene Hall, and discussing the young man's prospects with another guest. He made the remark, 'anyhow, Bob won't have to wait very long.' Lady Cardigan overheard the words, as her window was just above the speakers, and from that moment she made up her mind to outlive her husband's heir. This she managed to do by three years, for Lord Robert Brudenell-Bruce died without claiming his inheritance in 1912, after waiting for 44 years.

The title eventually passed to the Earl's second cousin, the Marquess of Ailesbury, so Adeline was the last Countess of Cardigan to live at Deene Hall. This was, and is a beautiful, fawn coloured, Tudor mansion, which reminds the visitor of a medieval castle with battlemented walls and tower. Adeline continued there in great style, until her money ran out. Her carriage was very grand and was driven by two postilions, who wore red jackets and white breeches. Two footmen stood at the back (the footmen at Deene were always over 6 ft tall in Adeline's time) dressed in black tailcoats and scarlet breeches. In 1873 she married Count de Lancastre, a Portuguese nobleman. It was not a successful marriage, for he did not like the country, did not shoot or hunt, and did not like the large shooting parties his wife arranged at Deene. After six years they parted, and the Count returned to Paris.

The Countess was always generous to her tenants, and Christmas was celebrated in the traditional way in the estate villages of Deene and Deenethorpe. A bullock or a park deer was killed and delivered to the inhabitants. The villagers were invited to tea, and an immense tree, decorated and laden with presents, stood in the White Hall. Carols were sung by the choir in the Great Hall in the evening and supper would be served to them in the housekeeper's room afterwards.

On audit days, when the tenants paid their rents, twice a year in May and November, they were sumptuously entertained at the Seahorse public house, formerly the White Hart. Each boy in the village was given a suit of clothes once a year, and every girl had a new dress and a cloak with a hood. Any cottagers who wanted nourishing soup could go twice a week and fetch it from the Hall kitchen.

Adeline became very friendly with the rector of Deene, Mr E.T. Sylvester, who lived at the Rectory, only she visited too often for the parson's liking. One day, seeing her coming to call from his study window, he hastily gave instructions to his parlour maid to tell Lady Cardigan he wasn't at home. When the maid opened the door to the visitor, Adeline refused to believe that the master of the house wasn't available and marched into the sitting room, where Mr Sylvester just had time to dive under the table, which was covered by a large cloth. Her ladyship was surprised to find the room empty and was nonplussed for a moment, but then she walked up to the table and banged it with her fist and said, 'It's no use Sylvester, come out! I can see your feet.'

As Adeline grew older she became rather eccentric and one of her more morbid fancies was to get her butler, Knighton, to measure her up for a coffin, many years before she needed it, and have it made up for her at Oundle. The Countess had it placed on a trestle in the lobby just off the ballroom. When the mood took her, she would have it carried into the hall and, wearing a blue silk dress, she would climb into it with the butler's assistance. Adeline would then ask the astonished maids how she looked in her coffin.

The Countess loved to receive callers even in her old age. One day when she was about 87, there were two visitors from Barnwell Castle, Lady Ethel Wickham and Mrs Charles Montagu-Douglas-Scott. A footman led them into a room in which stood a large gilt chair. After they had waited for a long time, the double doors were thrown open and Adeline tottered in, gorgeously dressed in her peeress's robes and supported on each side by a footman. As she sank into the golden chair, she smiled at her guests and said, 'I'm quite happy, I've outlived Robert.'

The colourful, philanthropic and eccentric Lady Cardigan died in 1915 at the great age of 91, having lived for 47 years after the death of her husband. She had, however, reduced the wealthy Cardigan estate to penury. Deene Hall then passed to the Marquess's two grandsons, Ernest who was killed in 1917, and subsequently to George Brudenell-Bruce, and is still the cherished home of the Brudenell family.

15

The Railway Disaster at Wellingborough

ON Friday the 2nd of September 1898 at ten past eight in the evening, Wellingborough postman Thomas Smith placed a four-wheeled truck beneath the arch near to the entrance gates of the station. He intended to load the mail he had brought onto the truck and take it to the platform, but the truck started to move of its own accord and fell on the track. The postman, who had been unlocking the gates at that moment, bravely jumped down onto the line. Foreman Richardson ran to his assistance and together they tried to lift the truck clear, but it was firmly wedged between the rails.

The Manchester express, which had left St Pancras at 6.45 pm and, after stopping at Bedford, was due to pass through Wellingborough very shortly, was this evening a few minutes behind time. As it approached the station the driver was probably trying to make up the lost time, so it appeared to be travelling at more than 60 miles per hour. It was seen, rushing round the bend, by the guard, Mr Heath, who was waiting to take the slow train to Northampton. He ran down the platform and waved a red light at the driver of the express, who clapped on the brakes.

Richardson and Smith tried frantically to remove the truck, but it wouldn't budge. The two men only just had time to escape with their lives as the massive engine bore down on them at a tremendous speed. The postman managed to

scramble onto the platform, and the foreman dived under the buffers of a train which was waiting in the station.

The express crashed into the truck and smashed the woodwork into fragments, the ironwork becoming entangled with the front portion of the engine. The train reached the end of the platform and at this point the engine left the rails and ran over the siding. It then ploughed up the embankment and turned round completely, smashing into the centre of the

train. One of its buffers penetrated a dining car. The saloon after the engine was empty and this was overturned on the main line and partly wrecked. It was very unfortunate that the next section, which was composed of six third class compartments, contained a number of passengers. This carriage was practically telescoped and the roof was lifted off and fell on the main line near to the tender. Very soon afterwards the shattered timbers ignited and it all became engulfed in flames.

A vivid picture of the crash was given by one of the passengers on the train, Mr George Spicer of Dover. He described how he saw 'a huge body crashing along the metals, which landed alongside their car. It was the engine. The sounds of splintering timber and the crashing of glass was accompanied by the piercing shrieks of men, women and children. The compartment filled with steam, which obscured everything, and for a time everyone was stupefied, not knowing what had happened. Then somebody shouted "make for the windows", and there was a smashing of glass as the passengers cleared a way through the glass panels. The interior was a wreck, with tables and chairs overturned and the floor strewn with wreckage of every kind.'

The express driver, Edwin Meadows, was killed instantly. His neck was broken but, strangely, the watch which he wore on a long chain around him continued to show the correct time. His stoker, William Joyce, sustained severe injuries, with a great wound to his head and a smashed thigh, and died an hour later in a waiting room. The bodies of a young man, Mr Richardson, and a woman, Mrs Butler, both from Leicester, were taken to another waiting room. Two of the passengers with the worst injuries were Miss Clark of King's Norton and Mr Dix of Derby. Miss Clark died at Wellingborough during the night and Mr Dix died a few hours later at the Northampton Infirmary. This brought the total number of people who died in the crash, or shortly after, to six, with nearly forty people injured, some of them seriously.

Wellingborough fire brigade, with their horse-drawn engine, managed to get near enough to stop the fire from spreading. News of the disaster soon spread and a large crowd gathered. Dr Audland hurried to the station on his bicycle, and his partner, Dr Hollis, quickly followed. Three other doctors together with ambulancemen and clergymen, worked through the night helping the injured passengers.

As there was no cottage hospital in Wellingborough at the time, a special train was laid on to take casualties to Northampton Hospital. Some of the less seriously injured were accommodated in the station house and looked after by Miss Turner, the eldest daughter of the station master (who happened to be away on his annual holiday).

The express train's driver and his stoker were both from Leicester and the two men were buried in the same grave in Leicester cemetery, a great number of railway men attending the funeral, appalled at the tragedy.

Mr Spicer's graphic eye-witness account makes chilling reading as he conveys the horror of being at Wellingborough station on that fateful September evening.

16

Watercress Harry

HARRY Wood was a colourful character who roamed around Kettering and the surrounding countryside at the turn of the century. He came from Leicester, where he had been a well-known boxer, but had been compelled to leave the town in a hurry for romantic reasons. Although he was these days 'an inspector of milestones', he made a frugal living by selling watercress, knowing where it grew for miles around. He would collect it in his basket and sell it in many of the towns and villages in north-east Northamptonshire. Harry became known as Watercress Harry and, when visiting the yards and backs of the terraced houses, he would shout, 'Watercress, Watercress, all fresh'. The children would run out from all directions, carrying their plates for a pennyworth of watercress.

Harry wore an old frockcoat and bowler hat and, although he was dirty and unkempt, he was always polite. Everyone said he was 'a gentleman'. Sometimes a housewife would save him some Sunday dinner and he would sit outside to eat it, come rain or shine, for he would never go into a house. He would always say, 'Thank you my love, and God bless you.' He rarely begged, but earned just enough to live on by his own efforts, although he had a weakness for alcohol and often spent his hard-earned money on beer.

One tale that is told of Watercress Harry is of how he got

caught taking watercress out of a stream on a private estate by the landowner. The squire, knowing that Harry sold it to make a few bob, took pity on him and asked him if he'd like to do a couple of hours' digging to pay for what he had taken. Harry cheerfully agreed and got on with the job. When the agreed time had expired, he picked up his basket of watercress and went on his way.

In the winter Harry would go to the outlying farms and cottages to sell oranges to the inhabitants, carrying the fruit in a large hessian sack. This was very popular with the children. At other times he would go into the wood and collect moss for use in wreaths, and get a few pennies for his trouble.

He would sleep rough, very occasionally taking shelter in the workhouse at Kettering and it was only towards the end of his life that he stayed in lodgings. This fine old character died around 1912.

In the 1980s his memory was honoured in the town when a public house was named after him. Although the former Gaiety, in Market Street, has since had another name change, and is now called Manny's.

17

The Friendly Invasion

GRAFTON Underwood is an attractive sleepy little village, with a stream, where ducks dip and paddle, running down the main street, crossed by bridges. The cottages are mostly of the 17th and 18th centuries, built of stone and with roofs either thatched or of Collyweston slate.

The church of St James the Apostle is hidden behind tall trees and, inside, a stained-glass window is dedicated to the memory of the American airmen who lost their lives in the Second World War, whilst serving at Grafton. The window depicts a B-17 'Flying Fortress' and has the words 'Coming Home'.

A splendid granite memorial a quarter of a mile out of Grafton, on the narrow lane leading to Geddington, states, 'The first and last bombs dropped by the 8th air force were from airplanes from Grafton Underwood'. The roadside stone and the lovely window in the parish church are among the few reminders of Station 106, which made such an impact on the small community when the air base was occupied by the United States servicemen.

The site covered 500 acres and was the first airfield to be available for an American airforce unit under the 'lease lend' arrangement when the United States entered the war in 1941. The 3,000 personnel were catered for in every way, with a hospital, chapel, cinema (the Roxy), mess hall and clubs, built

in a variety of Nissen huts and brick buildings situated amongst the woodlands on the Duke of Buccleuch's estate. A lovely setting, but in winter the ground crew renamed the airfield 'Grafton Under-mud'. On 6th July 1942, the 97th Bombardment Group (Heavy) moved onto the base, with its remarkable B-17s, designed by Boeing in 1934. The 'Fortresses' were over 75 ft long and weighed more than 30 tons, when laden with bombs. They needed a crew of up to ten to fly them, but had the great advantage that they could keep flying when badly damaged. The last unit to move to Station 106 was the 384th Bombardment Group (Heavy), on the 25th May 1943, and this remained on the site until the end of the hostilities.

When the GIs (so called because of their Government Issue) landed in this country, it was as much as a culture shock to them as it was to the British. They found a land where the lifestyle was very austere compared to their own way of doing things. The average wage in Britain was £2 at the time, and the slogan of the day was 'make do and mend'. It was hard to provide enough to eat with the meagre rations of 4 oz of bacon and butter per person each week, 12 oz of sugar for each person a week and only one egg per fortnight. In many ways, though, this was a fair system, treating everyone alike. All children received daily milk, orange juice and codliver oil, and people even got used to spam and dried eggs. Petrol was non-existent, except for the most essential of journeys. There were no streetlights, and every window was blacked out in case a glimmer of light might help enemy bombers. It was a time of sirens and Anderson shelters. Only the simplest of clothes were available, and even they could not be bought without coupons. Gas masks, and identity cards and only 4 inches of water in your bath were the order of the day.

The Yanks, having found themselves in Grafton Underwood, as quiet a place as you would unearth anywhere in England (it didn't even have a pub), set about discovering a means of enjoying themselves. The local bus company ran a late night service from Kettering, 4 miles away, and often there would be as many as 70 men to pick up on the last bus back, half of them having to push it up Warkton Hill. It was not unknown for many of the town's bicycles to disappear after the Americans had enjoyed a late night out drinking or dancing – the bikes would turn up the next day in the hedges near to the airfield. Local girls were swept off their feet by these handsome, confident GIs in their smart uniforms, and there were always plenty of them to fill the free trucks sent around the nearby towns and villages to take them to dances on the base. The men also took advantage of the weekly outing to the large town of Northampton (called the Liberty Run) when they were granted exit passes.

The Americans were quick, too, to learn where the nearest pubs were and they livened up the sleepy Northamptonshire villages, when they cycled out to look the places over. The Star at Geddington was a favourite haunt, as was the Three Cocks at Brigstock. Another pub that they used to frequent was the Vane Arms at Sudborough. This is a quaint, thatched building, and inside over the inglenook fireplace in the main lounge there is poignant reminder of those times. For, wedged in the cracks of the wood, are dozens of coins (mostly pennies) which were put there by the American airmen as a token of good luck before they went on a bombing raid over Europe. If one of them was killed in action, his friends would flatten the protruding bit of the penny over as a permanent reminder of the lost airman. There used to be about 200 coins in the great beam, but their numbers have dwindled, because customers have been known to take them home as souvenirs.

Some years ago a film called *The Memphis Belle* was made, and it gave a vivid portrayal of the heroic deeds of the American aircrew in their B-17s. The 384th bombardment

Group built up a reputation for heroism and dedication to duty while they were stationed at Grafton Underwood, and over 1,000 personnel received the Distinguished Flying Cross. In their 'fortresses' they carried out 9,348 credited sorties, lost 1,559 personnel and 159 aircraft, but claimed 165 enemy aircraft.

Although many of the local people at first resented the American arrivals and their brash new ways, they soon welcomed them with gratitude, as it became more and more obvious what a crucial part they were playing in turning the outcome of the war in our favour.

18

The Big Freeze

THE winter of 1947 was one of the coldest on record for nearly 70 years. The heavy falls of snow and freezing conditions went on for many weeks. From the 22nd January until March 17th snow fell somewhere in Britain for a record-breaking 55 days.

On the 26th February after five weeks of sub-zero temperatures one of the options that the government was considering was coal rationing. The availability of fuel had already become so acute that many factories and mills were on short time. The lack of coal had curbed supplies of electricity and gas, making four million workers idle through power cuts – and yet there was more than sufficient stocks of coal at the pits. The trouble was that because the roads and railways were blocked with snow the coal could not be moved. Many households were without light or heating during February, whilst many people in offices, shops and pubs carried on working – by candlelight.

Alice Smith (née Burnage) of Kettering could never forget the 22nd January 1947, the day her daughter Madeline was born. Alice was expecting her third child and the evening before it was particularly cold. At about 11 pm her contractions started and she asked Roy, her husband, to fetch the midwife from what is now the Stockburn Clinic, off London Road, Kettering. He had promptly set out on his bicycle as, in common with many they had no phone. When he got back his fingers were so cold that they were blue.

When the midwife arrived it had yet to start snowing. The baby was born two hours later at 2 am the next morning. All through this time her husband was worried in case the gas ran out, it was on a penny meter which also provided the light, but he needn't have worried because the gas lasted out.

At about 3 am the midwife left but came back a couple of minutes later to ask Mr Smith to help dig out her car (she had an old Morris Minor) as it was half buried in the snow. He managed to get the car out for her but that was just the start of the terrible winter of 1947.

It seemed to go on for weeks. Most of the men, including her husband Roy, were laid off because the lorries transporting the leather for the shoe factories could not get through – many of the roads were impassable.

For the Smiths it was a real struggle for them to make ends meet and try and feed the family. They burnt old shoes and leather offcuts to keep warm. They had an allotment off Gas Street (now Meadow Road) where they grew their own vegetables. Roy, and Alice's brother, Bill, decided to try and find some potatoes that they had set: they returned very down-hearted – they couldn't even get a spade into the ground let alone find any potatoes!

Alice remembers trying to take the baby out (in those days they were taken out for fresh air come hail or shine) but the snow was far too deep even to push the pram along. It was six weeks before she could get out with her new baby.

During this time the Smiths were living at 30 Northall Street (a supermarket car park is there now) and they had no mains water connected to the house having to fetch it all in a bucket from a tap at the top of the garden. The tap was often frozen and before filling the buckets they had to take boiling water up the garden to thaw it out. And of course the privy was also at the end of the garden! Alice now tells her grandchildren about that winter of '47 and says she can remember it as though it was yesterday.

Doreen Allen of Woodford, was living in Kettering in 1947 at Oak Road and attending the Rockingham Road girls school. As the great freeze went on and on, all schools were re-classified as requiring domestic fuel. Any coal that did get through went straight to industry and the schools soon ran out of fuel.

Doreen can quite remember walking to school and not knowing if they would have a full day. After registration and prayers the girls would have to dance in the school hall just to keep warm; while the caretaker went to the coal merchants to see if a supply of coal had come in over night. On his return the answer was always the same 'sorry, no coal today'. This brought a great 'Hurrah!' from the pupils, because it meant that they could go home.

At home the little coal people had was saved for the evenings. The electricity supply was cut off between 9 am and 12 noon when it came on again for an hour. This gave Doreen's mother a little time to cook a quick meal, but not enough for something like stew and dumplings which was what they really needed to keep them warm. However her mother got over the problem by asking the next door neighbour to cook their stew for them, as she had gas and was given 6d (2.5p) for her trouble.

Doreen's father was a scaffolder on a building site but this industry was an early casualty of the weather. However, when the storms abated her father got plenty of work clearing the snow, which was by now piled high by the roadside. The council paid laid-off workers to load the snow into lorries which rumbled through the frozen streets out into the country to dump it. This was a seven day a week job and it lasted quite a few weeks. Her father said he had never earned so much money in his life!

Here are some interesting snippets of news from the local *Evening Telegraph* of February 5th 1947 . . . 'Cold weather has driven wild deer from Hazel Wood, in Corby and they are feeding from the farmers' hay and pea stacks, during the recent freezing conditions' . . . February 8th. 'Every town in this area is severely hit by the dramatic decision to close down factories as a result of the fuel crisis now facing the country' . . . 'At Kettering more than 5,000 shoe workers and 2,000 clothing workers are affected . . . Cinemas will open for two nightly performances . . . Rushden and district. Eighty boot factories employing 12,000 people will be at a standstill . . . At Wellingborough practically all main factories are closed . . . At Corby the cuts may cause the temporary closure of part of the massive steel manufacturing plant of Messrs. Stewart and Lloyd.'

Hazel Payne (née Longhurst) of Kettering also has a very vivid memory of that winter and one of the most important days of her life. It was the 22nd February, her wedding day. Hazel was to be married at Cransley church, at 2 pm. She lived with her parents at Home Farm Lodge, three miles from the church and up a winding track beyond Cransley Wood. She was one of nine children, being the eldest girl. The day before the wedding only a little snow had fallen, but they awoke the next day to find huge drifts of snow everywhere. They had to dig out a path as best they could. A small car took some of her family to the church, but the larger wedding car booked for Hazel and her father got stuck in the lane. There was nothing for it, the bride-to-be and her father would have to walk to church. Hazel put on her wellingtons under her long white dress. Hazel's father had a pair of new leather boots on and kept slipping over, and so did Hazel but they both could not stop laughing about their predicament. It was a long three miles to walk to Cransley church, but eventually they made it and they were only three quarters of an hour late. Only a few local people managed to get to the reception at Broughton village hall, and of course there were no photographs because the photographer had got stuck in the snow. Although everything had gone wrong on her special day, Hazel can now look back on her wedding day with fond memories and much amusement.

John Letch of Corby, remembers that terrible winter very well, he was 12 years old and lived in New Town Row, Raunds with his parents and three younger brothers. During the first blizzard it snowed so heavily that when they opened their front door, (the terraced house had no back door) they found that it was completely blocked by a wall of snow. The only way they could get out was through a bedroom window. Several hours later they managed to clear a way through the snow-drift to their front door by using shovels and garden spades.

There were 14 houses in the terrace and John remembers a great community spirit as the neighbours helped one another through that difficult time. It took his father Daniel and his four young sons two days to dig their way out to the road. The snow was ten feet deep in some places and they had to use short ladders to dig huge blocks of snow out of the snow face. It was hard work but the boys thought it was great fun.

The local farmer who lived further up the Roman road towards Chelveston was completely cut off, only the tree tops could be seen sticking out of the snow-drifts. John's father decided to try and take some food to the farm, and he and John took the children's sledge and piled it with provisions and headed towards the farmhouse. They had no idea where the road was, so they pulled the sledge between them over the tops of small trees, hedges and farm gates. The two of them made for the smoke coming from the chimney of the farmhouse. John and his father made this journey three times to take food to the farmer and his family.

Harold Johnson of Irthlingborough can well remember how he came back to England in the September of 1946 after being demobilised from the RAF after spending 3 years in the warm climate of Southern Rhodesia as a flying instructor. Whilst awaiting a place at a teacher training college, he spent 4 terms at the little all-age school of Aldwinkle, where he taught the senior pupils, all twenty of them!

His journey to work consisted of a mile long cycle ride to the station, twenty minutes on the Northampton to Peterborough line from Irthlingborough to Thorpe with another mile long walk across the valley to Aldwinkle school at the other end. His return journey included a ride in the school bus. On the first day of the big freeze no trains ran on the line at all, so he stayed at home. On the following day the train took him as far as Thrapston where it was forced to stop and Mr Johnson then had to walk three miles through very deep snow, arriving at the school in the late morning. The headmistress and the few pupils that had managed to get there were very pleased to see him. After that and for the next six weeks his journey returned to 'normal', but the mile walk was usually carried out in bright sunshine but in sub-zero temperatures. This final part of the journey went along a raised wooden footpath over the road which was often flooded but which was three feet above normal ground level, now however this was on a level with the 3ft deep snow which lay all around.

The classroom in which Mr Johnson taught had no heating. The pupils and teacher worked for as long as possible until their hands and feet became so numb that they could stand it no longer. Then they would go outside and do PT, largely running and jumping on the spot. Only returning to the classroom when their circulation had improved.

Dorothy Lewin lived at Woodford Mill with her parents and sister Audrey. Dorothy's father worked for Mr Bream, at Woodford Lodge Farm, and was the last miller to grind flour in the 1940s. The mill was demolished in the 1960s. Dorothy can remember when the first heavy snow of 1947 came they awoke to find that the snow had covered all the ground floor window panes and the drifts were higher than a five-bar gate. They had to dig through one drift to get to their drinking water from a well. A dozen pigs were kept in four stys and these had to be dug out before they could be fed. A 6 ft snow-drift filled the yard and covered the entrance to the pig's feeding station. The cattle in the yard needed watering too, but before this could be done the girls' father had to dig a track along the garden wall which was 150 yards long with snow up to shoulder height, so that the cattle could be driven to the mill pond to drink. After that he had to break the ice on the pond each day as well.

The girls did not go to school for a fortnight, and the family was reduced to their last bag of flour, with just enough bread to last them for a few days. Luckily their mother always kept a well-stocked store cupboard. After being snowed in for two weeks and after the daily ritual of feeding and watering the animals, Dorothy and her parents decided to try and force their way to the village, about two miles away. Audrey stayed at home to keep the fires burning and have the lunch ready for when they got back.

The roadway itself was obliterated and the snow formed one large slope from the river's edge to a ploughed field at the top of a bank. They found the best way was to set off across the middle of the field, across and over the hedges and wall. It was very tiring trudging through the deep snow, and it took them an hour to get to the Co-op stores in Woodford. When they got there they found that the manager realizing their plight, had sent bread and provisions down to Thrapston, to be put on the first available train for an unscheduled stop at 'their' level crossing. Trains were at least managing to operate a reduced service.

Jean Parker of Rothwell was 12 years old in 1947 and had
a very unnerving experience in that bitter winter. Jean had
just been discharged from Kettering hospital, in the middle of
February, after having a kidney removed, which was a major
operation in those days. On the way home she had to be taken
to Thorpe Underwood by ambulance, which was as far as the
vehicle could manage. Jean recalls the great snowdrifts as they
headed towards Harrington, 'They looked like huge white
walls on each side of the road.' When they reached the field
gate she had to be transferred from the ambulance to a hand
stretcher which had two large wheels, one at each side.
Ambulance men had to push the wheeled stretcher half a mile
across the fields to where she lived. Jean would have loved to
have played in the snow but as she had recently been so poorly
she wasn't allowed out and could only watch the snow falling
from her sick bed.

Just when everybody thought the worst was over and spring
was just around the corner, the county took another great
battering when the blizzard of the 4th March struck the
country.

There was not a town or a village in Northamptonshire that
escaped the great blizzard which started on a Tuesday night
and continued right through the next day and all through
Wednesday night. It left a trail of destruction behind it and
was the worst blizzard in living memory. Wellingborough,
Rushden and Market Harborough were cut off from Kettering
by heavy snow. Hardwick and Bozeat were completely isolated
yet again. In most cases roads were not only blocked by deep
drifts of snow but abandoned vehicles often closed the roads as
well. On Strixton Hill near Wollaston, 12 lorries were
completely snow-bound. The drifts were so high that in some
cases they completely obliterated the hedges.

On Friday the 7th of March it was reported in the local
Evening Telegraph that 170 inhabitants of Caldecott, in the

Welland Valley were enduring their third day of isolation. The villagers were virtually living on milk which could not be taken away from surrounding farms. Bread and other provisions, however, were running dangerously low. Caldecott was surrounded by drifts of snow up to 10 ft high and claimed to be the hardest hit of all local villages. Upper Benefield was another isolated village. The inhabitants welcomed the arrival on the 6th March of eight local men and their six horses each equipped with panniers containing loaves of bread, which had been driven four miles across the fields from Brigstock, in shoulder high snow. The whole return journey took them six hours.

In Gretton a tragedy occurred when Owen Joyce of West End, was found frozen to death in a field in Wood Lane on the Thursday morning. Mr Joyce, a victim of the blizzard, was very nearly home when he wandered off the road into a field. He had been off work for a fortnight with influenza and Wednesday, 5th March, had been his first day back at work. He had left Messrs. Stewart and Lloyd at 4.30 pm and had tried to get a bus back to Gretton. When he realized that the buses were not running he started to walk home in steadily worsening conditions.

In the morning when he still hadn't arrived home, his niece, Dorothy Whitworth, asked the neighbours to help her look for him. Another Gretton villager, Mr Perkins, had passed him on the road from Corby on the Wednesday evening, as they struggled through the deep snow. He was probably the last person to see him alive. The search party soon found his frozen body in the field where he had lain all night, with the gale whipping round him.

Dr Trevor Hopkins, the headmaster of Bishop Stopford School in Kettering, recalls a family tragedy from the March of that fateful year. His aunt and uncle, Arthur and Edith Copson, lived on the Green at Scaldwell. His uncle had once been a butcher at Billing and at Spratton and in the war he had been manager of a Northampton egg packer. Their son Walter was born in 1923 and grew up to become a shepherd and cattle hand with over 1,000 ewes, lambs and steers in his control. Walter was about to become engaged and have his own farm. He loved animals and was very proud of his flocks and herds. During the March of 1947 he was busy digging ewes and lambs out of the snow drifts and on one occasion worked for almost 30 hours non-stop. When he returned finally to Scaldwell he collapsed with a cerebral haemorrhage thought to be caused by the extreme cold. No ambulance could travel beyond Brixworth from Northampton, so a farmer took Walter to Northampton hospital in the back of a trailer, filled with straw, and pulled by a tractor. He died the next day on the 6th March, aged 23.

Gordon Wells of Isham, remembers that bitter winter of 1947 when as a young policeman, he was living at Welford on the western edge of the county, near Rugby. His beat consisted of Welford, Naseby, Sibbertoft and three other hamlets. He was married to Irene and they had a small daughter, Brenda. On the day of the first blizzard in March he had been working for four hours in the morning, and was back at work again in the evening from 6 pm to 10 pm. He had been out on his cycle, his only means of transport, and at about 8 pm he realized that the weather conditions were getting worse. Gordon arrived home at about 9 pm and put his bicycle away for the night, then went down the road to see how things were. At 10.15 pm he saw the headlights of a car approaching slowly from Northampton on the A50. By this time the heavy snow had become a real blizzard and the car seemed to be making progress when all of a sudden the headlights shot up in the air at an angle of 45° 'like a pair of search lights'.

The driver, Freddy Bell, the proprietor of the garage at

Welford, was a man of habit and every night at 8 pm he would set off in his car from Welford for the pub at Cold Ashby to have a quiet drink or two. When Gordon saw the lights suddenly go up in the sky, he surmised that it might be Freddy Bell. His guess was correct; Freddy had driven straight into a frozen snow drift, and the front of his car was now pointing upwards. Freddy was not a fit man, being an asthmatic, so it was decided that Gordon would go back to the village, get a tractor from Freddy's yard then tow the car back to Welford. By this time it was about 2 am, so after a stiff whisky at Freddy's house, the policeman went home.

The next day they awoke to a completely white landscape with huge drifts of snow. In some places one could touch the telegraph wires with a spade. Welford was at a standstill and as most of the male population were employed by GEC at Rugby and no company buses or trains were running, everyone stayed at home. Local farmers, most of whom produced milk, could not get their product away from the village, so it was poured down the drains. On this particular day every road into the village was blocked by snow. Gordon went to see the village butcher, Mr Martin, who was also chairman of the parish council. They discussed the matter but Mr Martin could offer no assistance, so the policeman said he would go and telephone the county surveyor. After Gordon had explained the situation, the surveyor agreed to pay for local labour at two shillings (10p) an hour. The village bobby went around the three pubs in the village and recruited most of the adult males for the job of clearing the roads and digging out the snow. They started the next morning at the church and worked on the roads towards Northampton, Market Harborough and Husbands Bosworth. It took a fortnight to clear these roads, before eventually the snow-ploughs broke through and finally liberated Welford.

19

Coco the Clown

THE clown capital of the world! A surprising statement to make about a tiny village in the north-east of Northamptonshire – but this is what you would have encountered if you had visited Woodnewton on the 25th September 1994.

The date is the anniversary of the death of Coco the clown, who lived in the village in his retirement and died in 1974. In the six years between 1988 and 1994, three Clownfests were held, when clowns from all over Britain descended on the village, and thousands of people had the time of their lives.

It all started when Woodnewton was highlighted in a national report focusing on the worrying plight of essential services in rural England. The post office, shop, Methodist hall and pub (now, happily, reopened) had all closed, and a group of villagers decided to do something about getting a social centre in the village where all age groups could meet. The cost of building a village hall was high, even with grants, and when the appeal fund was set at £22,000 the committee began to think that they had set themselves an impossible task. They reached the first year's target by holding quizzes, sponsored glides and treasure-hunts, but the prospects of getting their new centre built seemed to be in the far distant future.

That is, until Helen Rowland, Coco's eldest daughter, came

to the rescue. Mr Bernard Moore (alias Mr Woo, the clown), a committee member of Clowns International, was visiting Helen, and she mentioned that the children's swings and slides in the village were beginning to be in need of repair. Her father had donated money for the original playground equipment from some work he had done on road safety, visiting schools and hospitals and combining serious matters with fun and laughter. Mr Moore volunteered Clowns International to help raise money for the playground, but, after he heard of the need for a new village hall, this project was also included.

The three festivals each began with a memorial service at Nikolai Polakovs' (Coco's) grave at midday, and this was followed by a grand parade of clowns, marching bands, juggling acts and the performance of the clowns, with a fun fair, fairground organ, morris men, and many other entertainments. All in all a village extravaganza and a fitting tribute to one of the world's greatest clowns.

Thousands of pounds were raised towards the final cost of £95,000 needed to build the new hall and to repair and maintain the playground equipment. The splendid social centre which the Clownfest Committee and villagers worked so hard for was opened by the internationally famous star of screen and television, Norman Wisdom (a life member of Clowns International) on Saturday, 17th October 1992. A plaque in the hall commemorates the event. The third Clownfest was held to raise additional funds for the new centre and charities supported by Clowns International.

Nikolai Polakovs was born in the Ukraine on the 5th October 1900, in the property room of a theatre where his father was property manager. He ran away to the circus at a very early age and became apprenticed to Rudolfo Truzzi, a well-known Italian circus proprietor who had settled in Russia. Truzzi suggested to the young man that as he had

91

acquired a number of skills such as juggling and acrobatics, and consequently was a jack of all trades and master of none, he might as well become a clown. He also said that Nikolai should take the pseudonym of Koko, using the syllable which occurred in both his forename and surname. This spelling was changed to Coco much later, when he came to England.

In the First World War, Nikolai served as an outrider in the 11th Siberian regiment, and in 1919 he met Valentina. They married and raised six children, two sons and four daughters. In the 1920s he worked in Germany on stage and screen, also performing in the ring of Circus Busch. While in Berlin he was offered a job in England and he joined the Bertram Mills circus in 1929, moving to this country in the December of that year. It was the beginning of a long career in his adopted land, whose people took the very funny man to their hearts. With his shock of red hair, which stood up on end, his sad expression, long loose coat, baggy trousers, gigantic shoes and belisha beacon walking stick, he was a flamboyant and outrageous character in the circus ring, but in his private life he enjoyed simple things, especially being surrounded by his family. His interests were classical music and snooker, but his passion in life was making people laugh and, above all, he loved children. Helen tells of an incident in Sheffield, when he was asked to visit a young boy who lay in a coma in hospital. Coco returned very upset and when asked by his wife and daughter what the matter was, tears ran down his face, which still had his clown's make-up on. He told them about the boy and said, 'what do they expect me to do. After all, I'm only a clown.'

Each summer Coco toured Britain with the circus and entertained in the ring at Olympia in the winter. In the Second World War he served in the Pioneer Corps, before joining ENSA to entertain the troops. He was dedicated to road safety and was awarded the OBE for his efforts in this field. In 1950 he wrote his autobiography, *Behind My Greasepaint*.

Bertram Mills' Circus closed down in 1967, and two years later Coco and his wife went to Woodnewton to retire, living in their caravan in the back garden of their daughter Tamara and son-in-law Ali Housani's house. It was a day that the locals are not likely to forget, when a large pantechnicon towing a caravan, and Valentina's large collection of pots and plants, including a bay tree, arrived in the village. Helen was a frequent visitor to Woodnewton at this time and liked it so much that she eventually went to live there. Helen recalls that her father was a strict disciplinarian and expected his children to persevere with their circus training. Each of his sons followed him in his profession as a clown. Helen worked with her father in the circus at a very young age, and later became an actress and cabaret artist.

Coco hated to be away from the ring and was tempted to join the Robert Brothers' circus at the age of 69, but the work became too much for him and his health suffered. He returned to Woodnewton, where he died, aged 74 years. His wife died in 1983, aged 82 years. They are both buried in the churchyard cemetery in Woodnewton.

As for Clowns International it was founded in the early 1930s by Stan Bult, and was originally called the International Circus Clown's Club, Coco being one of the founder members. By the 1960s the circuses had declined so much that the organisation changed its name to admit clowns in all fields of entertainment.

The society of clowns come together annually at Holy Trinity church in Dalston, London, for a service and a meeting. Their original meeting place used to be at St Paul's in Pentonville Road, but the church was demolished and the site was turned into a memorial to the great clown Grimaldi and called Grimaldi's Park. Clowns are known to the circus people as 'Joeys' as a reminder of Joseph Grimaldi. Until recently, Holy Trinity church housed the famous Motley Egg Collection and the Clown's Gallery. As each clown joins the organisation he or she must have the design of their face make-up (motley) registered. Every clown has to have a different motley and a replica of the design is put on an egg. The Gallery and Egg Collection became too large to be kept at the church and has now been transferred to Hillman Street, at the rear of Hackney Town Hall.

As the circuses have declined in numbers, clowns have diversified in their work and now perform at large functions, such as carnivals, or show arenas, as private entertainers. They also undertake a large amount of charity work, especially for children. As a spokesman for Clowns International stated, they were particularly proud of the part they had played in helping the villagers of Woodnewton to raise so much money for a village hall and playground. It was also a tribute to the memory of one of their past members, that most popular of circus entertainers, Coco the Clown.

Bibliography

Vaux of Harrowden Godfrey Anstruther.
History of the County of Northamptonshire Vol I John Baker, 1822.
Shire County Guide, Northamptonshire Jack Gould. (Shire Publications Ltd, 1988)
The History of Whilton Clive Haynes, 1975.
Northamptonshire Tony Ireson. (Robert Hale, 1954)
Northamptonshire Past and Present Vol I 1948-53 'The Affair of the Grafton Underwood Feast' Gyles Isham.
Northamptonshire Past and Present Vol II 1954-9 'Tales of Whittlebury Forest – Two Famous Prize Fights' C.D. Linnell.
Northamptonshire Past and Present Vol IV 1966-71 'Thomas Thornton at Astrop Spa' Christopher Tongue. 'Lawrence Washington, The Builder of Sulgrave Manor House' George Washington.
The Pytchley Hunt Past and Present H. Nethercote, 1888.
The Brudenells of Deene Joan Wake, 1953.
Rockingham Castle and the Watsons Charles Wise, 1891.
The Northamptonshire Village Book NWFI. (Countryside Books, 1989)